Made in the USA
Middletown, DE
09 October 2023

40460430R00057